Original title:
The Pinecone Parables

Copyright © 2025 Creative Arts Management OÜ
All rights reserved.

Author: Robert Ashford
ISBN HARDBACK: 978-1-80567-217-3
ISBN PAPERBACK: 978-1-80567-516-7

Folklore of the Forest

In the woods where whispers play,
A squirrel named Chuck had much to say.
He wore a hat, too big for his head,
Claiming he was king, though he never led.

The rabbits giggled and danced around,
While Chuck declared, "I wear this crown!"
A parrot squawked, "You're just a nut!"
And Chuck replied, "Just wait—I'll strut!"

The trees all shook with laughter loud,
As he tried to waddle, feeling proud.
But tripping on roots, he fell with a thump,
The log he landed on gave a big jump!

Then came a fox with a sly little grin,
"Do you need a throne, your royal sin?"
Chuck shrugged, he laughed, then took a seat,
Amongst the leaves, he felt quite neat.

Shadows of the Pine

In the shadow of a giant tree,
A squirrel danced quite carelessly.
He thought he'd lost his nutting prize,
But found it staring from a pie.

A wise old owl hooted with glee,
"You've got it, buddy, can't you see?"
The nut was stuck beneath his hat,
He bowed his head, now quite a brat.

Fragments of a Forest Fable

A chipmunk wore a tiny shoe,
He strutted proud, oh what a view!
He stepped right out on a big log,
And slipped right off—it was a fog.

The frog laughed hard, a croaky sound,
"In style you fell! You danced around!"
The chipmunk blushed but took his leap,
"Next time I'll stick, not run, then creep!"

Nature's Little Chronicles

A hedgehog rolled into the fray,
Proclaiming, "Today's my grand display!"
He pranced about, full of delight,
Until he tripped, oh what a sight!

A rabbit snickered from nearby,
"With all those spikes, you can't fly high!"
The hedgehog chuckled, undeterred,
"Just wait and see, I'll have my turn!"

Unraveled Myths of the Pines

A pinecone claimed it held the keys,
To secrets whispered by the breeze.
It wiggled, jiggled, made a fuss,
"Listen close, I know more than dust!"

Yet in its strive for fame and cheer,
It rolled not far; oh dear, oh dear!
With all its claims, it tumbled down,
And landed hard, all lost its crown.

Brooding Under Branches

A squirrel sat on a branch, chubby and round,
His stash of acorns could surely astound.
He wore a monocle, quite dapper and neat,
Meditating on snacks, oh what a treat!

A bird nearby chirped, "What's up with that guy?"
"He's plotting a feast, just watch as he sighs!"
The squirrel then gasped, a dramatic display,
"I'll conquer this brunch! Just get out of my way!"

Timbered Tales of Time

Once grew a tree with a curious face,
It cracked up the forest, a real funny place.
With stories of lumberjacks, so bold and so brave,
It tickled each leaf and every branch gave a wave.

The rabbits all gathered at dusk for a chat,
"Tell us a tale of that hat-wearing cat!"
In laughter they rolled, right next to the roots,
Imagining felines in fashionable boots!

Echoes of the Arboreal

In a glade where the laughter of trees fills the air,
A woodpecker knocks with rhythm and flair.
"I'm making a symphony! Can you hear it, folks?"
The owls just chuckled, their wise little jokes.

From branches to bushes, the whispers took flight,
"The nutty professor is here for the night!"
The fungi all danced in their caps and their gowns,
While shadows of critters turned up without frowns.

Seeds of Serenity

Beneath a large pine, a party was set,
With seeds and confetti, it's one we won't forget.
A hedgehog in sunglasses led the charade,
While dancing with mushrooms, who swayed in the shade.

As twilight approached, with stars shining bright,
The critters all sang, what a beautiful night!
With laughter and joy, they created a scene,
Where worries dissolved, and all hearts felt serene!

Treetop Murmurs

Squirrels chatter, plotting pranks,
Hiding nuts in leafy banks.
A crow with sass flaps overhead,
Next, a lizard steals the thread.

Branches sway like dancers bold,
Whispers of a tale untold.
A breeze tickles the tiny leaves,
Laughter echoes 'midst the eaves.

The Legacy of Little Seeds

Seeds with dreams of being trees,
Crack a joke upon the breeze.
A sprout declares, "I want to grow!"
While worms below put on a show.

Twisting roots play hide and seek,
While beetles boast of tales unique.
"Watch me bloom!" the flowers shout,
Unaware of weeds about.

Fables Upon the Forest's Edge

A rabbit raced, thought he was fast,
But tripped on roots, fell at last.
The wise old owl, with twinkling eyes,
Said, "Patience wins, oh little spry!"

Foxes danced in silly hats,
While badgers snored, dreaming of chats.
In the shade, the ferns confide,
"Life's a play, we're all the guide!"

A Symphony of Silence

In stillness, whispers come to play,
The grasshoppers join the fray.
Ants march in a silly line,
Planning feasts, all things divine.

Mice exchange the juiciest tea,
About the cat that couldn't see.
And in this quiet, laughter grows,
In nature's play, silliness flows.

Ruminations of the Rustic Realm

In the woods where squirrels play,
Pinecones gather, all in dismay.
They hold wisdom, or so they say,
But mostly they wish to roll away.

A chipmunk laughs at their grand tales,
While perched upon a bed of snails.
"You're just seeds of trees in jail!"
The pinecones grunt, "Okay, we fail."

Sunlight peeks through tree-top winks,
Pine needles dance as nature thinks.
The hoot of owls met with kinks,
Who knew life's truths were just in pinks?

Gather 'round, let us confer,
To share our laughs and make a blur.
With every chuckle, we prefer,
Helping forests with our witty spur.

Timbers of Truth

Branches stretch in funny ways,
Beneath the weight of sunlight's rays.
Twisted trunks on nature's stage,
Pinecones laugh at aging's phase.

Two pinecones argue over pine,
One claims the other crossed a line.
"I'm the star of this great design!"
"Ah, please, you just like to whine!"

The trees around all lean to hear,
As giggles rise and dimmed veneer.
Wisdom here is loud and clear,
The truth is silly, never drear.

So come and join this timbered jest,
Where every pinecone knows it's best.
Nature's humor puts to rest,
The notion life should be a test.

Divine Divinations from Decay

Beneath the trees where shadows lay,
Fallen pinecones gather to play.
They whisper secrets in a fray,
While bugs on duty scurry away.

One says, "What's it like to decay?"
"Feel free to try, it's quite okay!"
A beetle replies, "You know, hey,
I think you might need less cliché."

Leaves giggle as they dance in air,
While pinecones boast about their flair.
"Decay's just life, so please beware,
It leaves us all a bit more rare."

But truth be told in nature's game,
Decay just adds to life's great name.
Without it, life's a boring frame,
So laugh along; it's all the same.

Soliloquies of the Sapling

A little sapling tells a tale,
Of mighty trees who wouldn't fail.
"They all began from small and pale,
Yet here I stand, I shall not bail!"

Pinecones chuckle from the above,
"What do you know about being tough?"
"We're seasoned wise, and rough and gruff,
But, hey, you've got your dreams, that's enough."

The sapling sways, with prideful cheer,
"Each needle sharpens hopes sincere."
"Let's team up, with laughter near,
And spread our roots with carefree leer."

Together, they share a wish
To grow and laugh in every dish.
In nature's brew, it's quite delish,
Finding joy in every squishy swish.

Whispers from the Woodland Whisperers

In the shade of trees so tall,
Squirrels bounce and start to brawl.
One shouts loud, with nuts in hand,
"I'm the king of this great land!"

Then the owl hoots, wise and stout,
"You know, my friend, there's always doubt.
Losing acorns in a race,
Doesn't make you royal, just a nutty case!"

Pinecone Prose and Poetry

A pinecone rolled, a story told,
Of windswept days and a heart of gold.
Dancing in circles, it spun so bright,
"Watch me go! I'm a bird in flight!"

But a curious beetle stopped in his tracks,
"Rolling around, you'll need some snacks!
Why not sit down, take a break?
Life's not a race, for goodness' sake!"

Quests from the Quiet Glade

In the glade where whispers gleam,
A frog dreamed of a mighty scheme.
"I'll leap over every log,
And be the fiercest, coolest frog!"

But splashed by a stream, he fell quite flat,
The fish all laughed, "Look at that!
Your royal leap was more like a flop,
Better stick to croaking on that rock!"

Life Lessons from the Green Cathedral

In the grand cathedral, branches break,
A squirrel decides it's time to take.
"I'll build a nest on this high, high bough,
Nothing could stop me, oh, look at me now!"

But a gust of wind sent him whirling,
"Not so clever, look who's twirling!
Your lofty dreams just took a dive,
Stick to your ground, that's how you thrive!"

Nutty Narratives of Nature

In a forest of wonders, where squirrels conspire,
Acorns hold secrets, a nutty empire.
They chat about plants, like old pals at a bar,
Swapping tales of the ones who now travel afar.

A fox in a bowtie recites poetry grand,
While trees stop to listen, just as he planned.
Laughter echoes through leaves, a sweet serenade,
As mushrooms play hopscotch in sun-dappled glade.

The winds play magician, twirling leaves as they sway,
While rabbits hold meetings at noon every day.
Their agenda includes a new carrot trend,
With radishes featured, just 'round the bend.

So when you walk softly where giggles abound,
Remember these stories the critters have found.
Nature's a canvas of whimsical fun,
Where every creature's a poet, and laughter's the one.

Stories Beneath the Canopy

Beneath leafy arches, the critters convene,
With tales of mischief that sparkle and gleam.
A raccoon in pajamas insists he can fly,
While the angry old owl just rolls but one eye.

A skunk plays the banjo, its rhythms awry,
While the frogs in the pond scream, 'This tune's a big lie!'

They hop to the beat, causing quite the scene,
With laughter erupting amidst all the green.

Lizards tell stories of battles with shade,
Of daring escapes, and of games that they've played.
Squirrels join in, their voices they raise,
In harmony wild, they celebrate days.

So if you wander where the cool shadows fall,
Listen for giggles, the fun-fueled thrall.
For nature spills secrets, all wrapped up in cheer,
In every small story, new joy will appear.

The Ballad of the Spruce Seed

Once sprouted a seed with a whimsical dream,
To dance with the winds and to laugh with the stream.
'I'll grow up to be the tallest tree here!'
But first it must learn, and that was quite clear.

It trips on a rock, does a flip on its way,
Then gets snoozed by a deer, who just wanted to play.
The squirrel nearby only shakes its small head,
Saying, 'Dreams have their hurdles, but don't end up dead!'

Through sun and through rain, it stood oh so proud,
While daisies around formed a bit of a crowd.
With every mishap, there was laughter in tow,
Each tumble and trip made for quite the good show.

So join in the cheer for the sprout on its quest,
For nature is hoping, and truly, it's blessed.
With giggles and wiggles, let dreams take their flight,
In the heart of the woods, all stories ignite.

Guardians of the Green

In the thicket, a band of oddly clad trees,
Guard whispers of nature, soft secrets on breeze.
With hats of fresh moss and boots made of clay,
They gather at dusk for their nightly ballet.

The pine grins widely, spins round with delight,
While the oaks play their flutes, serenading the night.
A hedgehog in shades claps along to the tune,
As fireflies twinkle, a bright little boon.

They jest about seasons, the antics they bring,
The maple gets dizzy, it thinks it's a spring.
Yet laughter connects, through bark and through root,
In every old story, a tangible truth.

So heed all the laughter when strolling in green,
For nature's fine dancers paint scenes yet unseen.
In their quirky parade, there's joy and there's glee,
Just look for the guardians if you want to see.

Narratives of Nature's Design

In the forest where squirrels play,
Pinecones tumble, come what may.
One claimed it was a treasure chest,
For hiding acorns, it thought best.

A wise old owl hooted with glee,
'These cones are hats! Come look at me!'
The pine tree chuckled, swaying tall,
'Just stick around, you'll see it all.'

When the wind blew, cones took a dive,
'Now I'm surfing!' shouted five.
A family of birds squawked in fright,
Wings flapping wildly in mid-flight.

So next time you see a cone on ground,
Think of the parties that can be found.
Nature's jesters all unite,
In tales of joy, from day to night.

Conifer Chronicles

In a glade where the tall pines rule,
A cheeky cone decided to fool.
With a wink and a spin, it took a leap,
'Watch me roll down, I'm fast as a jeep!'

Beneath, the critters gathered 'round,
A race amongst cones? What a sound!
One tripped and tumbled, went off the track,
'Hey wait for me!' called a lost little pack.

A chipmunk chirped, 'You're quite the show!
Just beware of brambles down below.'
The cones laughed hard, gave a big cheer,
'With friends like these, we've got no fear!'

So if you wander through trees so grand,
Remember the cones, oh isn't it grand?
Their funny games and joyous fun,
In the embrace of the ever-funny sun.

Fragments of the Forest Floor

Among the roots, a gnome did dwell,
With pinecone hats, he looked quite swell.
'One day I'll rule the forest fair,'
He chuckled loud, with nary a care.

But cones rolled by with giggles and grins,
Each claiming they'd be the forest's twins.
A debate ensued on who wore it best,
While all the ferns laughed – what a jest!

A raccoon strolled by, all wide-eyed,
'What's this fuss? Is there a prize?'
The gnome just shrugged, with a wink and a frown,
'The winner gets to wear the crown!'

A shy little sapling raised its green hand,
'I just want to help, not to stand.'
That's how the forest learned so well,
Joy is best, when you freely dwell.

Myths Encased in Bark

In the woods of whimsy, tales unfold,
Where myths and legends are often told.
A pinecone warrior, brave and bold,
Claimed to guard secrets of ages old.

Yet on a sunny day with a gust of wind,
The proud cone lost its grip and grinned.
'On a whirlwind quest, I now must roam!'
The patchwork ground became its home.

Critters gathered, their eyes in delight,
'Is that a hero soaring in flight?'
With each tumble, they cheered so loud,
Nature's circus, how it made them proud!

So remember, when next you explore,
The tales of cones and forest lore.
For laughter echoes on forest trails,
In nature's heart, it's joy that prevails.

Chronicles of the Coniferous

In the forest, conifer chat,
A squirrel wore a funny hat.
He danced with glee, a sight to see,
While birds laughed loud from every tree.

The pinecones rolled, a game they played,
On downy cushions, nature made.
Each one a treasure, oh what a riot,
As critters cheered, 'Let's start a diet!'

A wise old owl with glasses cracked,
Said, 'These cones need a little tact!'
So they plotted schemes, in leafy guise,
To prank the fox, to their surprise!

But when they tried to pull their jest,
The fox just laughed, 'You're all a mess!'
They rolled in pine, a playful show,
In coniferous realms, fun's the way to go.

Tales of the Timbered Realm

A beaver built a wobbly dam,
While squirrels feasted on a jam.
They threw a party, nuts galore,
With dancing legs and laughter's roar.

The trees all swayed, a leafy band,
As critters sang across the land.
Raccoons showed up in matching socks,
With pinecone hats, they laughed in flocks.

A wise old tree spun tales of yore,
Of chipmunks rich, but needy more.
They haggled hard with generous ants,
While dreaming deep of nut-filled rants.

Yet all agreed that when the sun gleams,
Life's a party, full of dreams.
From roots to tips, in pine we trust,
In timbered realms, we laugh and bust!

Skeins of Nature's Wisdom

The pinecones giggled in a line,
As rabbits raced for dandelion.
They sang a song, off-key, but loud,
In nature's theater, they felt so proud.

A grasshopper jumped, mischief in mind,
While ants marched by, so perfectly aligned.
With every hop, a squeaky sound,
Made everyone laugh, joy abounds!

From wisdom shared in knots and rings,
To battles fought with fluffy wings.
The secret lies, oh what a jest,
In nature's laugh, we find our best!

So gather 'round, you woodland friends,
In the skeins of fun, the laughter blends.
From every twig, a story sings,
In the heart of nature, joy springs!

From Cone to Canvas

With cones in hand, they made a mess,
A painter squirrel, full of zest.
He splattered hues on every tree,
Turning nature into a jubilee.

A canvas wild, in colors burst,
As chipmunks critiqued, an art-filled thirst.
The works of art, so odd yet bright,
Made shadows dance in sheer delight.

A wise old fern with leafy flair,
Said, 'Art's not meant to be laid bare!'
So they hid their brush with stealth and wit,
To see who'd guess the art they knit.

In laughter's echo through the glade,
Their antics formed a grand parade.
From cone to canvas, you see, my friend,
Art's a journey, with no clear end!

Tales of the Untamed Trails

In a forest full of glee,
Bears tap dance on a log,
Squirrels jive with grace and flair,
While frogs croak a catchy fog.

A raccoon tries to steal a hat,
But ends up with sticky goo,
While owls hoot a silly tune,
Inviting all for a barbecue!

The trees sway with laughter bright,
As breezes play a game of tag,
Branches shake and roots take flight,
When a mouse dares to dance a wag.

Deer prance in polished shoes,
Chasing shadows through the night,
With giggles echoing like dew,
In the woods so pure and bright.

Legends of Lordly Larches

Once a squirrel sought a crown,
Made of acorns, proud and round,
He tripped on roots and fell right down,
Now he's known for wearing brown.

A wise old tree with stories vast,
Told of quests from days of yore,
But his branches broke with humor's blast,
When a curious bird asked for more!

Pinecones rolled like marbles under,
With laughter echoing like thunder,
Rabbits raced not for the prize,
But just to see the trees in surprise.

Lordly larches wave and play,
Holding secrets of the day,
With giggles trapped in every ring,
In the dance, new tales they bring.

Timeless Teachings of Trees

Amidst the leaves that chatter low,
A young sapling hears the call,
"Stand tall, be bold, don't fear the snow!"
As wise old roots begin to sprawl.

Raccoons argue over acorns fair,
While butterflies learn a new ballet,
Lessons brewed in the crisp cool air,
Nature's classroom, wild and gay.

Through whispers of the wind they seek,
Knowledge gathered from every branch,
And though the chatter may seem weak,
Even pinecones love to dance!

So here's to tales that trees have spun,
With laughter flowing like a stream,
Remember the fun, and never shun,
A world where branches brightly gleam.

Echoes of the Evergreen Enclave

In the nook of the forever green,
Where giggles sprout from shaded leaves,
The wisest pine has often been,
A source of jokes that never cleave.

"Why did the twig join the band?"
"Because it couldn't find a root!"
The laughter spreads like wild hands,
As every creature starts to hoot.

With each bark and chuckle shared,
The air is thick with playful jest,
Beetles sing, and flowers dared,
To join the company of the best.

So come and wander through this maze,
Of silly tales from every lot,
Where evergreen stories swirl in praise,
And pinecones remain the cherry on top.

A Dance of Dependence

In a tree, a pinecone shook,
It had a dance, but no good look.
The branches swayed, the squirrels twirled,
While seeds below kept dreaming, swirled.

A bird flew by, gave a loud cheer,
"You dance like you've got no idea!"
The pinecone blushed, then took a leap,
Now all the forest giggled deep.

The raccoons joined, with furry flair,
They did the coney twist in mid-air.
Fungi laughed from the dampened ground,
In nature's waltz, all joy was found.

They swung and spun, for what it's worth,
Creating chaos on this earth.
Oh, the mess of leaves and laughter,
Was it fun? Just look after!

Stories Seeded in Silence

In the quiet woods, a tale did grow,
From a seed that whispered, soft and slow.
It spoke of mischief in every tree,
A plot so funny, wild, and free.

The ants held meetings, plotting at night,
To steal a snack, what a silly sight!
But one brave snail tripped on a root,
And the grand plan went askew, to boot.

High up above, the owls hooted wise,
"What's cooking down there, oh dear spies?"
They chuckled low with a knowing glance,
As trees above joined in the dance.

So every night, the stories grew,
The laughter spread like morning dew.
With every tale, a chuckle bloomed,
In nature's heart, pure joy resumed.

The Guardian of the Grove

A sentinel pine stood tall and proud,
Guarding secrets, all nature's crowd.
With branches wide, it looked around,
And chuckled softly, without a sound.

The critters came with gossip to share,
Whispers of danger, of mismatched hair.
"Did you hear? The raindrops have feet!"
The tree just swayed, maintaining its seat.

A fox asked, "Why do you never run?"
The pinecone quipped, "I prefer the fun!"
While shadows danced and the sun played tag,
The guardian smiled, no need to brag.

And in its shade, a party began,
With acorn hats and a nutty plan.
Each creature cheered, under boughs so wide,
In laughter and stories, they'd forever reside.

Nature's Fragmented Thoughts

Rustles in leaves, thoughts come and go,
Was that a whisper? Oh, just a crow!
A fragment of joy, or silly delight,
A thought in the breeze that took off in flight.

Mice debated cheese and a berry's worth,
While a beetle claimed it knew the earth.
"What's that smell?" the things began to bicker,
While a playful breeze made everyone snicker.

Toads croaked advice on the rhythm of rain,
Seagulls squawked back, "We forget the pain!"
Each tended to thoughts like scattered seeds,
Raising fine laughter from all those needs.

So in the wild, as thoughts tumble and swirl,
Nature's secrets giggle, twist, and whirl.
A cacophony of musings takes flight,
In every odd whisper, there's joy and light!

Whispers Among the Pines

In a forest, tall and grand,
Pines share jokes, oh so unplanned.
Squirrels laugh, they roll on ground,
While acorns bounce, a silly sound.

One pine claimed it saw a bear,
But it was just a tree with flair.
Owl hooted, "Let's have some fun!"
As pine needles danced in the sun.

Another shouted, "Friendship's key!"
"Especially with a bumblebee!"
They shared stories, tall as trees,
While buzzing bees hummed melodies.

So if you wander through the woods,
Remember laughter's in the goods.
The pines they whisper tales so bright,
In shadows where the sun takes flight.

Secrets of the Evergreen

Underneath the shady boughs,
The pines share secrets, and who knows?
A squirrel skims, puts on a show,
While toads croak out a little prose.

"Have you heard of the bear that jogs?"
The pine tree quipped amidst the fogs.
It's got some sneakers, bright and wild,
Running after a squirrel who smiled.

A wise old owl chimed in with glee,
"Nature's laughter's wild and free!"
Then all the trees began to sway,
As leaves danced like they're on display.

So come and sit beneath these pines,
Where laughter sparkles, sweet as wines.
They hold the secrets, strange and true,
In the woodland, shared by me and you.

Tales from the Forest Floor

On the forest floor, where shadows play,
Fungi giggle in their quirky way.
A pine cone whispers, "Look at me!"
Rolling 'round, feeling wild and free.

"Did you hear about the grass's dream?"
It wanted to win a solar beam!
But sunbeams laughed, "Oh, give it rest!"
As dandelions puff, they jest.

A pebbly stone, with wisdom rare,
Said, "Life's a prank, if you dare!"
And crickets chirped, "Join in the game,
Each wobble adds to our claim to fame!"

So laugh along with nature's crew,
In every spot, there's fun for you.
The forest thought, "This is the way!"
With tales that brighten any day.

Wisdom in the Woodland

In the woodland's heart, full of cheer,
A wise old pine drew all near.
"Gather round, my leafy friends,
For laughter here never ends!"

"Who's the funniest of the bunch?"
Asked the fern with a curious hunch.
"Let's have a contest, plant a seed!
First to bloom, gets to lead!"

So daisies chuckled, tulips too,
While mossy greens swayed gently, woo.
"I'll tell a joke!" chirped a bird up high,
"It's a jolly thought, you can't deny!"

The wise old pine with a grin so wide,
Revealed the truth that nature's pride.
"Laughs and whispers make us grow,
In this woodland, we steal the show!"

Woven Whispers of the Woodlands

In the forest, a squirrel danced,
Gathering nuts, he took a chance.
With each leap, a comic twist,
Nature laughed, none could resist.

The owls pondered, wise and old,
While chipmunks schemed, oh so bold.
A pinecone fell, the ground did shake,
"Who dropped that?" cried the wide-eyed snake.

Mushrooms giggled on the ground,
With every step, a giggly sound.
Fairies peeked from leafy nooks,
Reading silly, story books.

So if you wander through these trees,
Be ready for the funny breeze.
For nature's tales, both wild and free,
Are woven whispers, full of glee.

Enchanted by Evergreens

The evergreens held secrets tight,
As rabbits played in pure delight.
A bumblebee buzzed a silly tune,
Chasing shadows 'neath the moon.

A wise old tree began to chuckle,
At the antics of a young knight's buckle.
"Your armor jingles like a bell,"
The gnomes all laughed, and all was well.

Pinecones giggled on the floor,
Planning pranks for those who bore.
With every thump and every roll,
They crafted mischief for the whole.

A fox slipped on a slippery leaf,
Gaining humor, without grief.
Tales of joy, in nature's glow,
Where evergreen giggles always flow.

The Wisdom of the Woods

Amidst the trunks of ancient might,
The creatures chuckled, oh what a sight!
A rabbit spoke of life with flair,
"Leave your worries, just beware!"

The wise old owl spoke in rhyme,
"Don't rush through life, take your time."
But under the wise tree's shade,
A bumblebee's dance led to a spade.

A pinecone rolled, and rolled, and rolled,
Cracking jokes as it grew bold.
"Why do trees never get lost?"
"Because they always know their cost!"

Laughter echoed in the leaves,
As nature spun its funny weaves.
For wisdom here has a twist,
In woods where giggles can't be missed.

Forgotten Fables of the Forest

In the woods, a story lurks,
Of silly bears and quirky quirks.
A raccoon juggled nuts with glee,
While mocking the tall, proud pine tree.

"Why do trees never get bored?"
"Because they talk to every hoard!"
The rabbits cheered, in funny fights,
While ants planned spectacles of sights.

Each fern hid secrets from the sun,
With giggles shared, who's won, who's won?
A squirrel claimed the crown of jest,
In this woodland tale, he was the best.

With echoes of laughter filling the air,
Forgotten fables, laid bare.
So join the fun beneath the sky,
Where forest tales will never die.

Chronicles of the Cone

A little cone danced on a branch,
It wore a hat like a funny lil' stanch.
With a jiggle and wiggle, it caught a breeze,
Singing a tune that brought giggles with ease.

The squirrel laughed, what a silly sight!
'You'll fall for sure!' he barked with delight.
But the cone just twirled, full of carefree cheer,
Claiming it had no worries or fear.

A breeze pulled tight, it spun all around,
As birds joked, "Don't get lost on the ground!"
But the cone just winked, a rogue with a plan,
And landed on soft grass like a true rockstar man.

Now tales of the cone fill the woods and the air,
Of how it danced like it hadn't a care.
So if you see it, give a chuckle or grin,
For that little cone always welcomes a spin!

Echoes of Nature's Secrets

In the woods where whispers play,
The pine cones gossip, come what may.
'Did you hear about the acorn's dream?
To sprout up tall and reign supreme?'

The owls hoot, exchanging tales,
Of squirrel pranks and windy gales.
"No way!" says one, with eyes aglow,
"Did you spot the frog in a snow-white bow?"

Meanwhile, the cones chuckle in glee,
As shadows dance on the old pine tree.
With secrets shared under starlit skies,
Nature's theater brings laughter and sighs.

So if ever you wander, just pause and listen,
You might catch the giggles that nature's dismissin'.
With each rustle and caw, the joy's on repeat,
Nature's own joke, oh, so sweet!

The Lost Lore of Coniferous Dreams

Once a legend spoke of a cone so grand,
It ruled the forest with a comical hand.
It wore a crown made of twigs and moss,
And led a parade—oh, what a chaos!

Said the bees with buzzing, 'Here comes the king!'
While the branches bowed, it did a funny fling.
The leaves sang songs while the mushrooms cheered,
As the proud little cone danced, totally revered!

Then came a wind with an audacious blow,
That scattered the cones like confetti in tow.
Yet instead of worry, they all had a laugh,
Claiming their dance was a nature-made staff!

Now the tales still spin through the pines and the bends,
Of that regal cone and its ever-great friends.
For in the wild, where the laughter streams,
Even the tiniest cones can fulfill big dreams!

Beneath the Canopy's Embrace

Underneath the great pine trees,
The pine cones giggle in the soft, cool breeze.
They whisper secrets with a hearty cheer,
Sharing wisecracks that only they hear.

One cone claimed it could fly like a bird,
Its friends all chuckled, thinking it absurd.
'I swear I'll soar!' it puffed with pride,
But flipped on a breeze and tumbled beside.

"Fear not!" called the next with a jolly grin,
"For all of us here, everyone gets a spin!"
The laughter erupted, as joy filled the air,
In their playful kingdom, free from all care.

So next time you wander beneath leafy heights,
Listen closely for giggles on magical nights.
The cones with their humor, enchanting and bright,
Turn an ordinary day into sheer delight!

Reflections in the Resin

Once a cone, with a grin,
Said to the tree, "Let me in!"
"Your bark is rough, your humor dry,
But I'll roll 'round just like a pie!"

As it tumbled down the hill,
It bounced and chirped with joyful thrill.
"Catch me, catch me!" was its call,
But it got stuck, oh what a fall!"

So now it sits with a laugh so bright,
Stuck in layers, a funny sight.
Though time goes by, the cone stays still,
With tales that give everyone a thrill!

When you walk 'neath the towering sighs,
Look closer, you'll see the funny pies.
For in each resin, there's laughter stored,
Just ask the tree, it won't be ignored!

The Leafy Ledger

In a book of leaves, I found a page,
Where grasshoppers leap, filled with sage.
"Turn me over, it's quite absurd,
To find a frog that couldn't be heard!"

With each rustle, the stories unfold,
Of delighted ants that couldn't be bold.
They planned a dance, oh what a sight,
But tripped on seeds, much to their fright!

Then came a snail, with a hat so grand,
Claiming the title of 'Best in the Land.'
But oh, how slow, it took its time,
To win the race, though it seemed like a crime!

So when you ponder the tales they weave,
Know the ledger's filled, just take a leave.
For in each leaf, there's a giggle or two,
And the forest laughs, just waiting for you!

Branches of Belief

On a branch high above, a squirrel took flight,
Believing in leaps, it gave quite a fright.
It twirled and it swirled, a show for the crowd,
"Look at me, everyone!" it chirped out loud.

But mid-air it faltered, oh what a scene,
It landed on prickles, the jump was obscene!
The laughter erupted, from squirrel and seed,
"Who knew faith was risky?" Oh yes indeed!

So branches they wagged, with playful tease,
As the critters around shared jokes with great ease.
"Next time, dear friend, let's stay on the floor,
Where leaping and flopping won't lead to uproar!"

So remember this tale when you reach for the sky,
Believe in your jumps, but don't ask me why.
For branches may sway, but the ground's not a joke,
It's where all the best giggles are never bespoke!

Nature's Enigmas

In the heart of the woods, I met a wise owl,
Perching atop with a serious scowl.
"Why do leaves fall?" I asked with glee,
"To tickle the ground, just like me!"

The squirrel chimed in, with nuts in tow,
"Why do we run? You'll never know!"
And off it went, with a leap and a twirl,
Chasing its tail, what a whirly whirl!

The trees just chuckled, their secrets concealed,
While nature played games, their laughter revealed.
"What's green and talks?" a twig did inquire,
"The chatting beetle!" they said with fire.

So here's to the wonders, the giggles, the laughs,
In nature's great puzzle, with no little halves.
Each critter and leaf, all play their part,
To bring a smile to the wandering heart!

Stories Sown in Shadows

In the forest, whispers play,
Little critters dance away.
Squirrels chat about the rain,
While the hedgehogs shrug in pain.

Mushrooms giggle in their rows,
Tickling toes of passing crows.
A fox tells tales with a smirk,
Claiming he's the forest's clerk.

Down the path, a raccoon squeaks,
"Why do trees wear ancient creaks?"
A wise owl huffs, "Just for fun,
When they're bored, they strut and run!"

At twilight's end, the shadows flare,
And the logs take turns to dare.
"Let's play hide and seek tonight!"
"Only if you promise to fright!"

Woodland Wisdom

Beneath the leaves, they gather 'round,
Chattering wisdom, never profound.
A rabbit said, "Don't be so mean,
To a snail in his slime-green sheen!"

"Life's like a nut," the wise crow cawed,
"Hard on the outside, but tasty with gnaw!"
The deer paused, a twinkle in eye,
"Or just take a leap and see if we fly!"

Bats took notes in the moonlit air,
While frogs called out, "Life's never fair!"
"Just croak and hop," the otter chimed,
"Forget about all that heavy stuff rhymed!"

And as the stars began to wobble,
They laughed at their little woodland trouble.
From every tree to every shrub,
The forest thrived on a silly rub.

Echoes of the Ancient Pines

The timeless trees, they laugh and sway,
Sharing secrets of yesterday.
"Who dropped the acorn?" one tree sighed,
"I bet it was that mischief fried!"

The pines began to crack a joke,
"Why did the log refuse to poke?"
"Because it feared the dance of fate,
Or ending up on someone's plate!"

A raccoon jumped in with a grin,
"Pines drape blankets, thick and thin!
When winter comes, we dust with snow,
And the squirrels put on a show!"

From branch to root, the laughter grew,
Echoing tales both old and new.
In the grove of stories spun tight,
Nature's giggle echoed through the night.

Secrets in the Soft Earth

Deep in the soil, a worm once told,
"Life's a riddle, not just gold!"
A mole then piped, with a cheeky tease,
"Why don't we dig for some lost cheese?"

The beetles laughed, in cars of leaves,
"Don't be foolish, it's all just thieves!"
"Let's party down," a shrew began,
"Oh dear ground, you rock this plan!"

A tiny ant said, "I'm in! Let's roll,
Dance with me, it's good for the soul!"
With every poke from muddy clod,
They jived and swayed, praising the sod!

So if you wander near that patch,
And hear giggles in a soft hatch,
Know that secrets —funny and true—
Lie in between the earth's soft hue!

Beneath the Needle-Laden Sky

Beneath the sky with needles high,
The squirrels plot and loudly vie.
They scheme and dream, they dance around,
For acorn crowns they've newly found.

A pinecone rolls, the squirrels race,
Spinning 'round in a dizzy embrace.
They topple over, tumbling down,
With nutty giggles, they claim their crown.

The wind chimes in, a cheeky breeze,
While all the critters laugh with ease.
They twirl and whirl, a merry sight,
Beneath the trees, all feels just right.

Yet in the midst of all the fun,
A grumpy owl says, "I'm no son!
Not part of this wild, feathered show,
Just watch your nuts, or they might go!"

The Shattered Silence of Autumn

In autumn's hush, the leaves take flight,
A ruckus breaks the starry night.
A raccoon stumbles on a seed,
And starts a party, yes indeed!

The owls hoot out their dismay,
As all the critters join the fray.
With acorns tossed like little bombs,
They chuckle loud in joyful psalms.

A squirrel joins with his acorn stash,
He's getting tipsy, oh what a crash!
The forest floor's a vibrant mess,
With giggles echoing, no less!

Yet when the dawn begins to rise,
The party fades, to bright surprise.
The creatures scurry, hide from light,
To dream of autumn's stars so bright.

Cedars Sing Fables

In the woods where cedars stand tall,
They gossip low, they whisper small.
With stories old of critters' fun,
And legends spun when day is done.

A pinecone drops, and all ears perk,
It's time for tales, no one can shirk.
A sage-old squirrel shares a plot,
Of missed acorns and a winning lot.

The fungi giggle with delight,
As dawn brings laughter back in sight.
With every rustle, a story's spun,
Of twilight chases and acorn runs.

Each cedar nods their wise old heads,
As critters gather in cozy beds.
They dream of tales, of joy and cheer,
In the fun-filled woods, year after year.

Shadows of the Timber

In shadowy depths, where secrets hide,
The critters gather, side by side.
With whispers soft and giggles loud,
They plot their pranks, a raucous crowd.

A wooden stump becomes their stage,
Where every squirrel takes the page.
They leap and bound with tails held high,
In this timber circus, oh my, oh my!

A pinecone boasts, with a cheeky grin,
"Last week, I toppled a bear with a spin!"
The others roar, their sides do ache,
In shadows deep, they laugh and shake.

But as the moon takes center stage,
The party fades; it's time to gauge.
They curl in nests, with sighs of glee,
For timber tales will always be.

Echoing Wisdom of the Woods

In the woods where squirrels play,
Fables bloom in bright display.
A pinecone tumbled from a tree,
Said, "Why not laugh? Just be free!"

A wise old owl with eyes so round,
Told a joke still unprofound.
"What's a tree's favorite song?"
"Anything that's two woods long!"

Frogs croaked tales of blissful strife,
Making merry, full of life.
A teasing breeze began to swirl,
And danced with every playful girl.

The forest chuckled, hearts aglow,
As pine needles fell like show.
Nature giggles, so sublime,
In this comedy of pine and thyme!

Whispers of the Wild

Among the pines, the whispers start,
A pinecone chuckles, plays the part.
"Why did the tree refuse to bark?"
"It couldn't find a proper lark!"

A jolly rabbit hopped along,
Joined by birds in joyful song.
"What's a mushroom's favorite game?"
"Mushroom hunt, it's quite the fame!"

With vines that dangle, twist, and tease,
The forest giggles in the breeze.
Every leaf a secret shares,
Tickling our hearts with silly flares.

The shadows frolic, spirits lift,
Laughter woven as the gift.
In nature's arms, we find the best,
A wacky world we're truly blessed!

Rustic Reveries in Green

In a cozy nook of leafy grins,
A pinecone giggles, where fun begins.
"What did one acorn say to the tree?"
"I'll grow big, just you wait and see!"

A mice parade is having a ball,
Crawling around, they're small but tall.
"What's a tree's favorite hairstyle?"
"The one that makes it look quite versatile!"

With vines that dance and flowers that prance,
Each creature's got a story to chance.
The breeze composes a lighthearted tune,
As insects whirl under the moon.

Laughter blends with nature's sigh,
As chipmunks puff their cheeks up high.
In this comedy, we all belong,
Rustic reveries in nature's song!

Nature's Tapestry of Tales

From branches high, a giggle dropped,
A pinecone joked but never stopped.
"Why was the leaf so shy today?"
"It couldn't find its bright bouquet!"

Beneath the ferns, a chorus grows,
With whimsical tales of blissful prose.
"What do trees wear in a winter show?"
"Their coats of snow, a frostbit glow!"

The sunbeams wink, a playful light,
Dancing shadows, what a sight!
A flip-flop frog leaps through the reeds,
Cracking jokes, planting funny seeds.

Nature weaves her colorful threads,
With giggles woven in her spreads.
In this tapestry where tales are spun,
Life's a festival — oh, what fun!

The Journal of the Juniper

In a forest deep and wide,
Juniper scribbles, a scribbler's pride.
Telling tales of squirrels that dance,
Waving paws like some squirrel romance.

Every acorn's a plot twist told,
While ferns roll their eyes, feeling quite bold.
The dance-off of owls with sleepy eyes,
Leaves all around burst out in surprise.

Juniper writes with a twist of fun,
Spinning yarns till the setting sun.
The chipmunks giggle, the robins chirp,
As stories twist, twirl, and then burp!

So come take a peek, join the wild spree,
In the journal's tale of silly glee.
A forest of laughter, a woodland cheer,
Where stories tickle the ear like a deer!

Harvesting Hope in the Pines

In the Pines, hope grows tall,
Underneath the pinecone sprawl.
A gathering of critters, a festive sight,
Harvesting giggles from morning to night.

Squirrels with baskets, a comical sight,
Hoarding odd things, oh what a delight!
One found a shoe, another a hat,
They fashion a train, imagine that!

Their little parade, such rambunctious cheer,
A spectacle wild, as friends gather near.
The pines nod above, with a swish and sway,
As laughter spills out, in the sun's warm ray.

In every cone lies a story to find,
Of hope and mischief, of silly designed.
With each hilarious tale that they weave,
Expect nothing less than joy to believe!

Roots of Reflection

Beneath the tower of sturdy old trees,
Worms tell stories that tickle the knees.
Roots that twist and dig down deep,
Whispering secrets as they gently creep.

A wise old oak shares his best joke,
About a pumpernickel and a silly bloke.
The laughter erupts from the sage of the glen,
As branches sway, 'Do it again!'

Reflections ripple in the pond below,
Where ducklings float with a quack and a glow.
In every splash, a chuckle rides,
While cattails giggle and sway with pride.

Roots of the forest dance with delight,
With every amusing tale shared at twilight.
In this whimsical world, take a break,
And dive into laughter, for fun's sake!

Tapestry of Tree Tales

In the canopy high where laughter spins,
A tapestry woven of giggles and grins.
Branches of storytellers, just so spry,
Weaving rumors that float in the sky.

An acorn once dreamed it could be a hat,
While a breezy pine whispered, 'Imagine that!'
Singing songs of adventures so bright,
As the forest erupts, filling day with light.

Tales of a porcupine learning to dance,
With twigs for legs, and a prickle romance.
The laughter is ripe, it fills up the air,
In this crazy tree gig, everyone's aware.

So gather 'round close, listen and see,
The funny old stories that branch into glee.
A tapestry spun with threads made of fun,
Each tale grows a giggle, and the laughter's never done!

Lessons Written in Bark

In the woods where squirrels chat,
Wisdom grows beneath the hat.
A tree may teach with a creak,
But only if you dare to peek.

Raccoons read by the moonlight,
Laughing at the beaver's kite.
Nature's class is quite absurd,
With lessons noted in each word.

The ants take notes, they work in ranks,
While the fox just laughs at the pranks.
From every branch and twist of vine,
The forest writes its punchline.

So if you hear a twig that snaps,
It might just be the oak that claps.
Embrace the humor, let it flow,
In trees we find the best of show.

The Language of the Forest

Whispering leaves in gentle breeze,
Chatter of critters brings us ease.
A boisterous owl hoots a joke,
While the pine cones giggle and poke.

Frogs croak tales of yesteryears,
While ants recount their wildest fears.
The trees converse in playful rhymes,
As nature sings of silly times.

Mice share secrets among the roots,
And raccoons don their fancy suits.
Each critter dancing, swaying slow,
The forest's language steals the show.

So join the fun, do not be shy,
With every rustle, hear the sigh.
A symphony of laughter raised,
In nature's waltz, we are all praised.

Nectar of the Old Growth

Deep in the forest, humor flows,
With every drop, the laughter grows.
Old trees joke with a quirky twist,
A nectar sweet, you can't resist.

Bees buzz by with cheeky grins,
Pollinating all the forest spins.
They share puns with every flower,
Turning work into comedy hour.

The owls roll their eyes at night,
Claiming wisdom is a lofty flight.
But laughter drips from every bough,
Igniting joy in the old growth's vow.

So sip on this sweet forest brew,
Let the chuckles carry you through.
In each drop, a story unfolds,
Of laughter woven in the bold.

Reflections in a Pine-Scented Breeze

A breeze rustles through the tall pine,
With scents of laughter, oh so fine.
The forest chuckles deep and loud,
As critters gather, bold and proud.

Beneath the branches, antics bloom,
The woodland stage, a cozy room.
Chipmunks juggle pine cones with glee,
While the trees sway in harmony.

The fragrant air sparks witty tales,
Of woodland battles, silly gales.
Every gust carries a punchline,
In nature's glee, we all align.

So listen close to what you hear,
The laughter's close, it's always near.
In every whisper of the trees,
You'll find the joy in life's mysteries.

Echoes of Evergreen Dreams

In a forest where whispers were strong,
Pinecones giggled, a comical throng.
They plotted to roll down the hill,
Creating a ruckus, such joyous thrill.

Squirrels looked on with a chuckle and grin,
As pinecone shenanigans caused a din.
But the pinecones, oh, they stumbled and fell,
Landing smack-dab in a bird's cozy shell.

The birds, bemused, shared a laugh or two,
As pinecones danced round looking for dew.
With every small slip, they'd cheerfully shout,
"We'll be the best acorns, there's never a doubt!"

So if you stroll past the trees so tall,
Hear the laughter, and heed the call.
For pinecones, you see, are the soul of the fun,
In their world, the jokes have only begun!

Tales from the Conifer Corner

In the heart of the trees, where the shadows sway,
Pinecones told tales at the end of the day.
With stories of squirrels who danced on the breeze,
And knock-knock jokes that brought even bees to their knees.

They endeavored to prank every creature they could,
Rolling down hills, hoping to be misunderstood.
But alas, they collided with a wandering hare,
Who chuckled and joked, "Not a toy, I declare!"

The owls rolled their eyes, wise beyond their years,
While pinecones cracked jokes that put them in tears.
"What do you call a tree that's afraid of the dark?
A 'stump'—oh, the laughter, it hit like a spark!"

And so, in the corner where conifers stand,
Wisdom and whimsy go hand in hand.
With laughter and love, they spread good cheer,
These quirky pinecones, who persevere!

Wisdom of the Woodland

Amidst the green leaves where the sunlight bends,
Pinecones share wisdom with immediate friends.
"Don't worry too much," said one with a grin,
"Just roll with the punches, let the fun begin!"

They held a small meeting on a clear pine branch,
To teach all the critters the art of a chance.
"Life is like bouncing off rocks in a stream,
Sometimes you'll flop, but you might just dream!"

With laughter that echoed through bushes and vines,
The woodland critters formed silly line designs.
"Why don't pinecones ever get lost in the rush?
Because they stick close to the trees—they just hush!"

So, join in the laughter, let the timber jive,
In the wisdom of woods, we all can thrive.
Where pinecones scheme in their jovial glee,
The forest can be the best place to be!

Pinecone Testaments

Underneath the towering pines, taking a break,
Pinecones swapped stories, all for fun's sake.
"Ever heard of the one who flew like a ball?
Let me tell you, it wasn't for long at all!"

They met with chipmunks, who twitched in delight,
As pinecones recounted that memorable flight.
"Then down I did tumble, with a thud and a shake,
And landed right here, oh, what a mistake!"

The laughter erupted, a chorus of cheer,
With each little tale, their worries grew clear.
"Here's a great tip," said one with a wink,
"Just roll with your blunders—trust me, I think!"

So while they are giggling beneath the tall trees,
Pinecones remind us of life's little ease.
It's not just the journey that makes it all bright,
But the friends that we find in our whimsical flight!

Parables in the Pine Needle

A wise old pine whispered to me,
"Don't judge a cone by its scaly spree!"
Nature's humor coats each branch,
In the forest, life's a silly dance.

Squirrels giggled at their own show,
Chasing tails in a nutty flow.
The acorns laughed from the oak above,
"Who needs stardom? We've got love!"

The sap dripped slowly, a gooey laugh,
"I may be sticky, but I'm full of craft!"
Pine needles bristled, a green parade,
Waving like flags, in sunshine's fade.

So gather 'round, by the tall tree,
Let's share these tales, just you and me.
For in the wood, the stories weave,
With giggles hidden among the leaves.

Whimsy Among the Woods

In an ancient grove, the trees conspire,
With jokes and pranks that never tire.
A cardinal teased a crow with flair,
"You might be black, but I fly with rare!"

The pine tree's cones, they rolled and spun,
"Catch us if you can, it's all in fun!"
A chipmunk chuckled, tail held high,
"I'll eat these seeds and wave goodbye!"

A rabbit named Hazel held court supreme,
"Life's just a giggle, or so it seems!"
With a hop and a skip, she danced around,
Proving wisdom can come from the ground.

So gather your friends and join the fun,
In the wood, there's laughter for everyone.
Each whispering pine, each rustling leaf,
Tells a tale of whimsy, beyond belief.

Pinecone Lore and Legends

Once there was a cone, so round and proud,
Claiming height, above the crowd.
"Taller than the rest," it shouted clear,
While birds rolled eyes, and snickered near.

A sapling murmured, "What a sight!"
"I'm doing yoga, up to new height!"
Pine needles giggled in the earthy dyad,
"Flexibility beats pride; you know that lad!"

The forest floor swayed with a hearty cheer,
A toad croaked loudly, bringing good cheer.
"Life's just a tale of ups and downs,
With laughter shared among the towns!"

So if you wander down this path,
Where cones tell tales and giggle with wrath,
Remember the lore of the woodland glee,
In every whisper, a joke will be!

Murmurs of Mossy Memories

Beneath the pines, where moss has grown,
Lies laughter woven in every stone.
A mouse once squeaked, with a tiny yawn,
"Who needs a bed? The earth is my lawn!"

The slugs slid by, with a wink so sly,
"Why rush through life when you can slide by?"
With clarity that only slow can grasp,
Their slimy wisdom, made joy last.

Fungi giggled in their colorful hats,
"We're fungi, we're fun! No need for spats!"
While fireflies twinkled the evening's dim,
"We party here! Come dance on a whim!"

So stroll through the woods, take it slow,
Join the whispers, let the laughter flow.
In a mossy nook, where memories hum,
Life is a giggle, oh so fun!

www.ingramcontent.com/pod-product-compliance
Lightning Source LLC
Chambersburg PA
CBHW072143200426
43209CB00051B/331